BIRDS

OF NORTH AMERICA

BIRDS
OF NORTH AMERICA

PETER N. CASEY

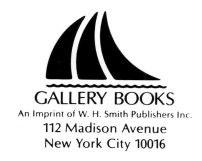

GALLERY BOOKS
An Imprint of W. H. Smith Publishers Inc.
112 Madison Avenue
New York City 10016

Back Cover. Tundra swans mate for life, and the young of each year stay with the pair until the following spring. This pair project a mirror image on the glassy surface of the water.

Page 1. During courtship, the graceful, long-necked western grebes will rear up vertically in the water and race one another side by side over the surface of a lake.

Pages 2, 3. Breeding in large colonies on islands and along the coasts of the North Pacific and North Atlantic, the common murre can easily be considered the northern equivalent of the penguin.

Page 4. These four spotted eggs will soon be four spotted sandpipers. Usually placed some distance from the water, the nest is built on the ground and frequently hidden by grass and other leafy vegetation.

Page 8. Next to the great horned owl, which has a slightly deeper call, the barred owl is perhaps our most recognizable hooter. It and the barn owl are the only owls with brown eyes.

CONTENTS

INTRODUCTION

From the rocky coves and tide-swept beaches of Atlantic Canada to the forested valleys and Rocky Mountain peaks of British Columbia, the splendid colors and the distinctive songs of Canada's bird population are a constant source of everyday wonder and delight. From the Point Pelee marshlands at the southernmost tip of the country, to the Arctic tundra and beyond, millions of birds make their homes here, while millions more visit Canada to nest or feed, or as a stopover along their migratory routes.

Indeed, of the estimated 8,600 species of birds in the world, and the approximately 650 species common to North America, more than 400 can be found in Canada year-round, or during some part of the year.

Our shores and oceans are rich with fish and other marine life required to support the large colonies of gulls, puffins, gannets and other coastal and sea birds that gather there.

Our rivers and lakes teem with food for the many types of waterfowl native to Canada—kingfishers, herons, ducks and grebes.

The grasslands of our western provinces supply nesting places and a diet of seeds and insects for prairie species such as the grouse, partridge and quail, as well as orioles and finches.

Vast stretches of forest and timberland provide a natural habitat for the birds that nest and feed high in the branches of trees, or in the ferns and moss of the forest floor. For hawks and owls, the forest is alive with small birds and mammals; and while autumn forests send warblers and other insect-eating birds to search for food in temperate, southern climes, jays, nuthatches, thrushes and numerous finches remain to feed on the abundance of seeds, nuts and berries that last in our woodlands throughout the autumn and winter months.

Even the inhospitable Arctic comes alive when its brief summer welcomes the annual arrival of Canada geese, phalaropes, arctic terns and other species that journey north to lay their eggs and raise their young while plants and sealife are plentiful.

Terns travel to their Canadian Arctic breeding grounds from Antarctic waters—a distance of some 14,500 kilometres (9,000 miles). They make that trip twice a year, returning to the Antarctic as soon as their young are mature enough to fly.

Such feats are not rare in the bird world. The arctic warbler migrates every autumn in one long flight across the Pacific to Formosa, while the willow warbler winters in Africa some 13,000 kilometres (8,000 miles) away from its Canadian home. The American golden plover leaves Nova Scotia each year to winter in Guyana and northern Brazil and makes that trip in approximately 48 hours. The bobolink, which breeds across southern Canada from Nova Scotia to British Columbia, winters in northern Argentina, Paraguay, western Brazil and eastern Bolivia.

Equally extraordinary is the behavior of those birds that inhabit Canada year-round. Flight, in itself, is amazing from a technical point of view; the distinctive habits of courtship and nest-building and survival techniques such as camouflage and deception are also intriguing to the bird-lover.

Birds benefit mankind in many different ways. They are our most efficient and effective allies against the clouds of insects that attack farm crops and timberland and that are a general nuisance in our outdoor lives. Hawks and owls eat rodent pests. Gulls and many other species are useful scavengers, while several varieties of birds live on the seeds of weeds.

For most Canadians, however, the true value of our birds must surely be measured in terms of the pleasure they bring into our daily lives—the sight and sound of them and the dazzling, effortless acrobatics of their flight.

Of all living things in the animal kingdom, birds are our most colorful and constant companions. For those who believe that spring is heralded by the appearance of the first robin rather than by an arbitrary date on the calendar, and for those who regard the call of a loon on a northern lake as the most beautiful sound ever heard, birds hold a very special place in the nature of things.

Since the beginning of time, birds have figured prominently in the art, mythology, religion, legends and songs of every age and culture. In folk and fairy tales they have been alternately depicted as harbingers of good or bad luck. They are a constant ingredient in the stories, songs and nursery rhymes of childhood and in poetry for all ages.

In North America there are an estimated 2,000,000 bird-watchers. This number continues to increase dramatically every year, perhaps due to an increased awareness of the importance of preserving the natural environment.

Our national and provincial parks are magnificent preserves in which bird-watchers enjoy the color, sounds and antics of Canada's birds. For many people, the annual migrations and the seasonal mating, nesting and feeding patterns of birds have become a source of great fascination. Entire vacations and annual outings are planned to coincide with phenomena such as the arrival of the gannets at their nesting grounds on Bonaventure Island, near Percé, or the filling of autumn skies with the formations and honking of Canada geese.

Bonaventure, off Quebec's Gaspé Peninsula, is one of many locations frequented by serious bird-watchers. Southwestern Ontario's Point Pelee National Park is another to which—armed with binoculars, spotting scopes, bird books and cameras—hundreds of thousands of visitors are attracted annually by the presence of wood warblers and many other species of birdlife nesting and feeding in the grassy marshlands or along the shore.

No first-time visitor to Vancouver should resist the opportunity to drive north of that city for a breath-taking view of the majestic American bald eagles that soar and hunt and nest along the steep mountain cliffs on the coast.

The pilgrimage to Grand Prairie, Alberta, to see wild trumpeter swans, or to Hawk Cliff near Port Stanley, Ontario, will be a lifetime memory.

Delta Marsh, the summer nesting grounds of the yellow-headed blackbird in Manitoba, and nearby Oak Hammock, populated by prairie and marsh birds in huge numbers year-round, are two more areas that will delight bird-watchers.

It isn't necessary, however, to set off across the tundra in search of gyrfalcon in order to enjoy the pleasure that birds can bring into our lives. Apart from the subtleties of habit, marking and song that distinguish the numerous varieties of hawks, warblers, swallows, sparrows, ducks and gulls, there are simpler joys to be found close to home—the variety of color that birds add to our world, the music of their songs, or the thrill of seeing an unfamiliar species attracted to a feeder stocked with seed or suet. The comical and awkward tug-of-war between a young robin and an earthbound worm would delight anyone. Along the seashore, children of all ages marvel at the graceful soaring of gulls; even in the deepest canyons of the cities we can chuckle at the busy crowds of pigeons.

This book presents more than 130 species of bird life, captured on film by some of the country's leading wildlife photographers. Here are the songbirds—the finches, warblers, sparrows and chickadees—that, as a family, make up more than half of all the birds in the world and fill the land around us with the music of their song. Here are the hawks, owls, ospreys, eagles and other birds of prey; the bitterns, herons, killdeer and sandpipers that populate Canada's shores; the loons, ducks, geese and other waterbirds that nest and feed on our rivers, lakes, inland waterways and along both coasts; and the woodpeckers, partridges and grouse of the Canadian forest.

From the marshlands to the mountains, from the southernmost regions of the country to the northern breeding grounds of the snow goose and the arctic tern, Canada's bird population is one of extraordinary and seemingly endless variety.

This young Canada goose will learn to
fly in about nine weeks and will soon
take its place in a honking migratory
V-formation southward.

BIRDS OF PREY

Whether skimming over marshland in search of field mice or other small mammals, plummeting in spectacular dives from great heights, or silently winging their way through the thick of night-time forests, birds of prey are among the most handsome and awe-inspiring members of the bird world. Well-equipped for hunting, with strong feet and powerful talons for grasping their catch and sharp hooked beaks for tearing flesh from bones, they are the natural enemies of any number of small animals, amphibians, reptiles, insects, fish and other, smaller birds. As a group, and in the overall balance of nature, they perform an invaluable service by keeping pesty rodent populations in check.

In recent years, the indiscriminate use of pesticides has proved a serious threat to many species, the toxic contamination of insects and small animals causing the birds to lay sterile or thin-shelled eggs that do not hatch. The magnificent American bald eagle was one species particularly affected; however, the breeding populations of this large fish-eating bird seem to have recently stabilized and appear even to be growing.

In all, there are approximately 260 species of birds of prey in the *falconiformes* order—the recognized grouping of hawks, eagles and harriers—with some 35 of these to be found in North America. All share the remarkably keen eyesight of the hunter, and most build large, bulky nests of branches, sticks, twigs and vegetation which they use year after year and build onto until the nests grow to enormous proportions. Bald eagles, because of the vast size of their territory, have been known to build two such nests, alternating between them year after year.

Among the most splendid of all birds of prey must be the osprey which, in addition to its magnificent aerobatics, is frequently seen snatching large salmon from the ocean or from the mouths of rivers after spectacular dives of 100 feet or more.

Equally fascinating in this world of graceful, yet fearsome hunting birds is the peregrine falcon which, while taking smaller birds in flight, has reportedly been clocked at speeds of up to 180 miles-per-hour.

The goshawk, while not nearly as swift, boasts an incredible maneuvrability that allows it to pursue smaller birds through the thickest of forest growth, something falcons cannot do.

The owl is undoubtedly the most recognizable of all birds of prey. Contrary to popular belief, owls have excellent daytime vision and at least three species—the snowy, the short-eared and the hawk owl—do most of their hunting during the day. In flight, whether hunting by day or by night, their very large wings and remarkably soft flight feathers permit them to float and pounce almost silently on the mice, frogs, birds, rabbits and other small animals that make up their diet.

Unlike the hawks, eagles and falcons, most owls build their nests in cavities in trees. This has made them more accessible and so more familiar to man.

Page 12. Most common along the Pacific coast, the bald eagle feeds largely on fish, which it catches near the surface of the water, finds washed up on beaches, or steals from the osprey.

Above. Although not a fast flyer, the long-winged northern harrier uses surprise as an effective hunting tactic when preying on rabbits, frogs, snakes and smaller birds.

Nesting on the ground close to salt or fresh-water marshes, the northern harrier is a prolific breeder, laying as many as five eggs, as opposed to the two or three commonly laid by other hawks.

Left. The American kestrel is the smallest and most common of the falcons. In many cities, where it often nests on the ledges of tall buildings, it is credited with holding in check the population of house sparrows.

Above. The spectacular plumage of the snowy owl, and its habit of perching conspicuously in exposed places, make it easy to spot on its infrequent visits to more southerly climes from its natural arctic habitat.

Previous pages. When fully grown, the red-tailed hawk will measure 20-26 inches in length and have a wingspread of 51-57 inches. Its nest, of sticks and branches, is often used year after year.

Above. Young red-tailed hawks can fly at about 45 days, and their parents teach them the art of hunting for at least several weeks, until they are capable of feeding themselves.

The red-tailed hawk, seen here in its dark phase, is a member of a magnificent hunting family; it spots its prey from lofty perches or while soaring in large circles high in the sky.

The largest of the falcons, the handsome gyrfalcon is seldom seen south
of the arctic circle, where it feeds on
ptarmigan, seabirds, ducks and small
mammals.

Not strong enough to do its own killing, the turkey vulture relies on its keen vision, watching the ground as it soars in search of carrion. Here an adult rests on its nest.

Left. Living entirely on fish, the osprey has feet and talons especially developed to grab and hold its prey while it flies off to its nest or feeding perch.

Page 26. Also called Richardson's owl, the boreal owl is very small and surprisingly approachable. If you are lucky enough to find one perching in low branches during the day, you may even be able to stroke its feathers without frightening it away.

Page 27. An extremely rare forest dweller, the northern goshawk is a close-to-the-ground hunter and the largest of the accipiters, a hawk grouping which also includes the sharp-shinned and Cooper's hawks.

Left. The small, tame and inquisitive saw-whet owl gets its name from its call, which is not unlike the sound of a saw being filed. It can often be attracted at dusk by a soft whistling.

Above. Enjoying a curious relationship with the prairie dog, the burrowing owl nests in small colonies of up to 12 pairs, often in the abandoned dens of prairie dogs or other burrowing animals.

The great gray owl nests in trees, and will often use the nests of other birds. Its distinctive large facial disks and long tail (for an owl) are characteristic features.

Known for its quavering, mournful call at night, the eastern screech-owl is the only small owl with ear-tufts. It is often found in trees in city parks, where it perches and sleeps in the daytime.

Right. One of the few daytime hunters of the owl family, the northern hawk-owl is easily recognizable by its long, hawklike tail and distinctive black "sideburns."

Slightly smaller than a crow, the
Cooper's hawk is a short-winged, long-
tailed woodland hunter.

Often violent in its defense of its nest and young, the female long-eared owl feeds the owlets with small mammals and amphibians caught by the male.

In almost any town or city in North America, the darting, erratic flight of the common nighthawk and its distinctive cry mean summer insects are being devoured at dusk.

Previous pages. Much smaller than the great horned owl, the long-eared owl has its tufts closer together on the top of its head. Superbly camouflaged, it can blend in completely with the tree in which it is sitting.

Above. The widely-spaced, horn-shaped tufts at the sides of the great horned owl's head are the predominant marking of this strong, ferocious and silent hunter of the woods.

Right. Ranging from Mexico to Canada, the prairie falcon feeds on small and medium-sized birds which it usually catches in flight.

SONGBIRDS

Probably no birds bring as much joy into our daily lives as the *passerine* or perching birds. Masterfully adapted through the evolution of their feet for perching, they live solely on land, the oceans and large lakes playing no part in their lives other than as among the major hazards of migratory flight. Known simply as songbirds to most of us, they are part of a grouping which makes up almost half of the approximately 8,600 species of birds in the world. Most birds in this large family have exceptionally well-developed songs.

These songs are put to use in many ways in the daily lives of the birds and throughout the seasons and stages of their lives.

Newly hatched, young birds use their 'voices' to encourage their parents to hunt for and bring food to the nest. They seldom stop calling until they have been well fed. As they mature, young birds appear to be coaxed from the nest and encouraged to test their wings by the reassuring chatter of the parents.

There are calls of alarm or danger that seem distinctly different for a mate, for young birds, or for other members of a flock.

And during periods of courtship, the male birds use their intricate songs to establish territory, to ward off other birds, especially other competing males, and, of course, to attract a female.

It is during this time of courtship and mating especially that the birdlife around us is at its most colorful and vociferous. It is then that we are surrounded by birds that appear to be singing for the simple joy of their own songs.

Most of us recognize a robin's song at the end of the day, or the persistent shrieking of the male cardinal at an hour that seems suspiciously ahead of daybreak. The loud chirruping of the English sparrow is familiar to even most city dwellers. We have become familiar with the mewing and the raucous kak-kak-kak of catbirds, the twittering of starlings and the complex clucking and whistling of blackbirds. We can, if we listen, learn to identify many more of the calls, trills and shrieks around us.

Page 38. The northern oriole's skillfully woven "sleeping-bag" nest can often be spotted hanging high in elm or other deciduous trees. The oriole feeds on insects, including vast numbers of caterpillars.

Above. As with many sparrows, the preferred habitat of the small, gray-breasted chipping sparrow is the edge of woodland, orchards and the gardens, shrubbery and lawns around houses.

Related to the robin, and similar in
size, the varied thrush sports a distinct,
broad, dark band of plumage across its
orange breast.

Left. The chunky evening grosbeak is another seed-eater of the forest who can frequently be a backyard visitor at feeders stocked with sunflower seeds.

Upper right. Also known as the English sparrow, the house sparrow is something of a bully. More aggressive than most of our smaller birds, it frequently usurps their nesting spots.

Lower right. A pair of yellow-throated warblers in breeding plumage tend their nestlings. Often difficult to spot from the ground, these beautifully colored little birds creep along the branches of trees in search of insects.

Although the house wren prefers to
nest in the wild, you may find it raising
its young in discarded automobiles,
woodpiles or abandoned sheds.

A northern nester, the Harris's sparrow
spends the breeding season in the
stunted growth between the treeline
and the edge of the arctic tundra.

Above. Smaller than the Bohemian waxwing, the cedar waxwing is a sleek, softly colored, crested bird that builds a loosely-constructed nest of twigs, grass and down near berry bushes or orchards.

Right. Anyone who has ever heard the penetrating, emphatic, early-morning song of the northern cardinal knows that this is a bird that is extremely proud of its own voice. The only all-red bird with a crest, the cardinal feeds on seeds, berries and insects.

Undoubtedly, the robin is familiar to more North Americans than any other bird. In many areas, the robin and its pleasant song have long been regarded as "the first signs of spring."

Like mocking birds and thrashers, the gray catbird is delightful to listen to and is a remarkable mimic of the songs of other birds.

A marshland dweller, the tiny swamp sparrow has a trill that can often be heard as he perches, hidden from view, in alders, cattails or lakeside shrubbery.

The brilliant scarlet coat and black wings and tail of the male scarlet tanager make it the most vivid of our songbirds. Roger Tory Peterson has compared its song to "a robin with a sore throat."

Similar to a warbler, but less active, the
red-eyed vireo, like all vireos, searches
for insects by looking under decaying
leaves on the ground rather than by
darting about.

The predominantly slate-gray and black loggerhead shrike is a robin-sized insect hunter who spots his prey from fence posts, telephone poles and wires.

Left. Like the red-wing, the yellow-headed blackbird is constantly on the move, foraging in grainfields, freshly plowed ground and barnyards, as well as in wet marshes and at the edges of lakes.

Above. Clark's nutcracker is distinguishable from Canada jays by the white patches on its black wings and tail. Its diet, which consists largely of conifer seeds, is sometimes supplemented with scraps found in logging camps or on farms.

Following pages. Four nestling barn swallows eagerly await the return of their parents who are off gathering insects; swallows catch their prey in mid-air in and around barnyards and suburban areas.

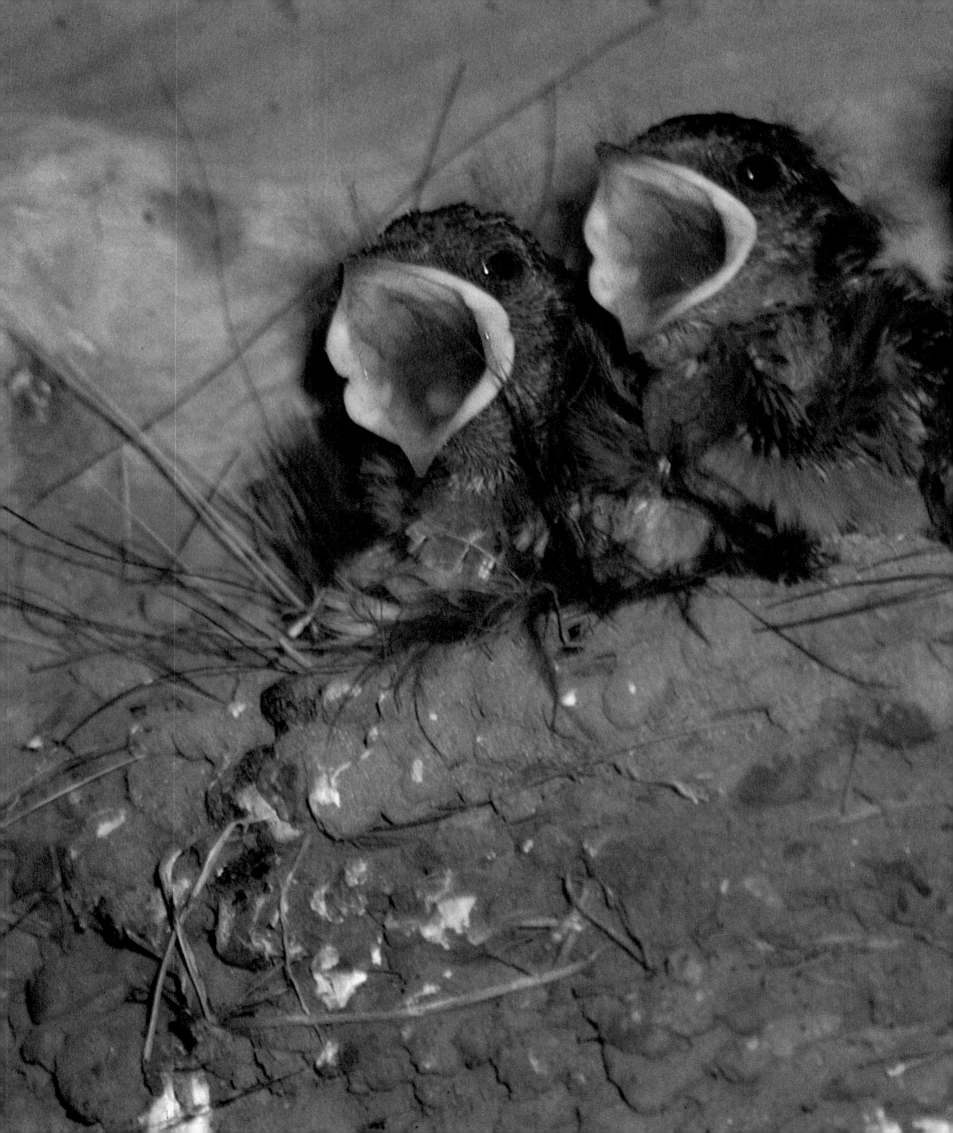

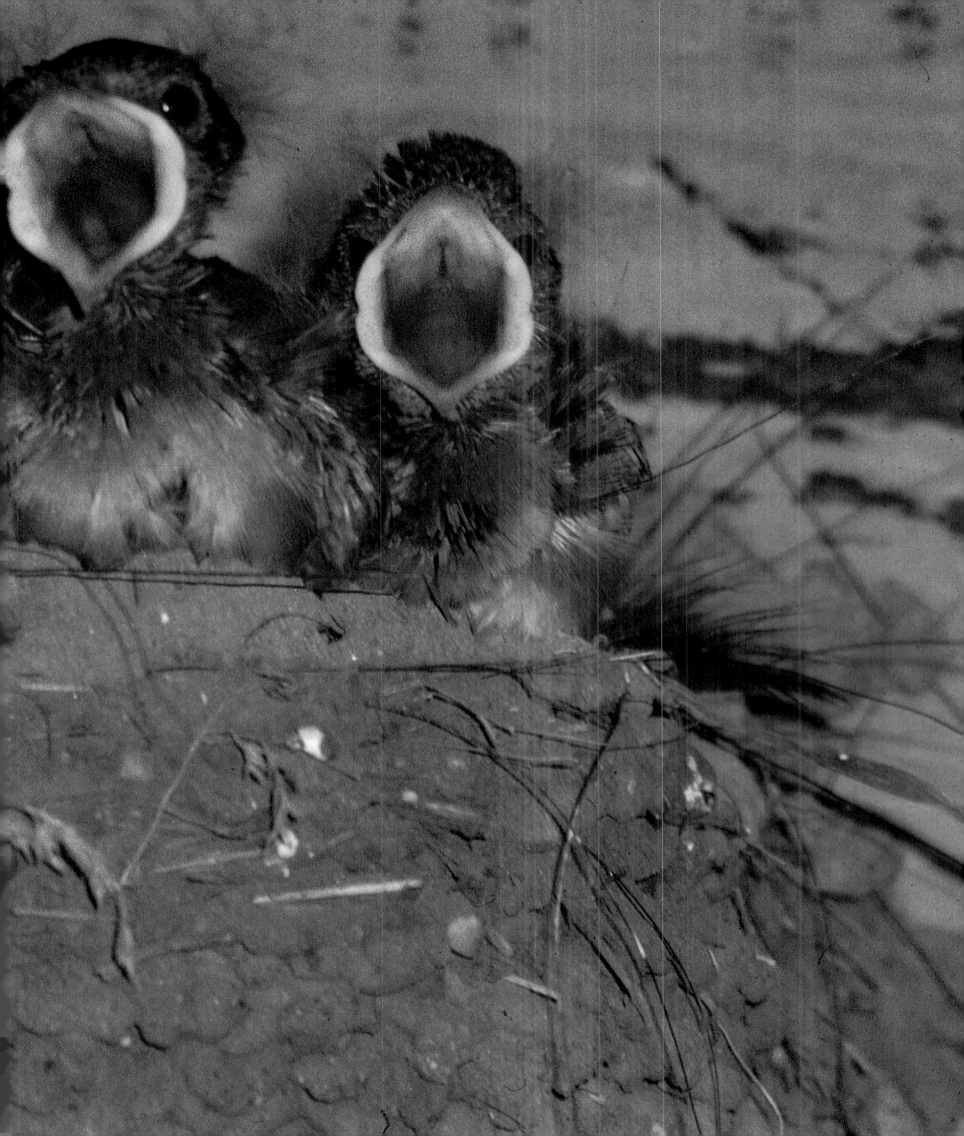

A truly beautiful bird in its coloring and flight, the barn swallow is so thoroughly comfortable nesting and hunting in the presence of humans that it will often nest on the rafters of verandahs and barns.

A young eastern kingbird devours a
dragonfly brought to the nest. The
adults hunt from posts or trees in open
spaces, catching their insect prey in
mid-air.

Flitting from perch to perch, the male red-winged blackbird is an energetic, cheerful sight in bulrushes, marshland and fields of grain stubble.

From the arctic islands to southern Mexico, the horned lark nests on the ground in open spaces, especially near weedy fields or shores. Tiny tufts of feathers on the head of the male resemble horns.

The striking blue of the male is a contrast with the grayish-brown coat of the female mountain bluebird. Unlike the eastern bluebird, the mountain variety does not have a rusty red breast.

The eastern and western meadowlarks are extremely difficult to tell apart on sight, the western having more yellow on its throat than the eastern pictured here. The western's rich, bubbling song, however, is in marked contrast to the high-pitched whistle of the eastern.

Above. Often called a wild canary, no other North American bird has as much yellow plumage on its back, wings and tail as the tiny yellow warbler. Although it prefers to nest in willows near water, it is commonly found nesting in gardens and orchards.

Right. The alder flycatcher adds its voice to the many birdsongs commonly heard in willow and alder thickets at the edges of streams and swamps. This bird is also known as Traill's flycatcher.

Above. The tiny American tree sparrow nests in the arctic, heading south in the winter, when it can often be seen with other sparrows and juncos around feeding stations or feeding on seed pods of dried weeds.

Right. Slightly larger than a sparrow, the eastern bluebird is the only bluebird with a red breast. It frequently nests in woodpecker holes, and can sometimes be attracted with nesting boxes.

The clear, plaintive song of the field
sparrow can often be heard in open
grassy or weedy areas, where the bird
feeds on insects during the summer
and the seeds of weeds throughout
the rest of the year.

Nesting in shrubbery or on the ground,
the song sparrow commonly hatches
three to five young. Its song is a
familiar sound. Its flight is character-
ized by the pumping of its long tail.

Left. Four eager beaks clamour for food as an adult grasshopper sparrow scans the dried grasslands surrounding the nest. When frightened, this small brown bird flies short distances, then drops into the grass like a grasshopper.

Above. Probably the most numerous of the wood warblers, the myrtle is one of the very few warblers that can live on a diet of seeds and berries for long periods of time. Its nest is lined with hair and feathers.

Above. A pair of Bohemian waxwings and their nestlings. The cup-shaped nest is made of twigs, lichens and plants, and will be home to the young, who are fed by both parents, until they learn to fly in 15 to 17 days.

Right. The only flycatcher with a feathery crest and a long, rufous tail, the great crested flycatcher is also noted for its loudly whistled "wheeep." It aggressively chases larger birds out of its territory.

Unlike the mourning dove, the
mourning warbler gets its name from
the sombreness of its dark gray hood
and black bib, rather than from its
song, which is loud and cheerful.

Right. The highly iridescent greenish-
blue or purple of the head, neck and
upper-breast plumage and the
yellowish-white eyes are the distinctive
markings of our largest blackbird, the
common grackle.

Young rose-breasted grosbeaks wait
expectantly for more food, while the
mother keeps a watchful eye. The
species gets its name from the male,
which has a distinctive V-shaped patch
on its breast.

The American goldfinch breeds in open areas of weeds and shrubs and on the edge of the woods. A lively feeder, its bright yellow summer plumage can easily be spotted darting about in flight or perched in trees.

FOREST BIRDS

The large coniferous forests and broad-leaved woodlands of this continent vary greatly from north to south and region to region, producing through the seasons of the year a kaleidoscopic range of habitat for all manner of wildlife.

During the spring and summer months, our northern forests are alive with plant, animal and insect life, and with the sounds of the birds that nest, feed and raise their young high up within the shelter of branches, or safely camouflaged on the forest floor. For many birds, these are seasons of abundance, with swarms of insects everywhere, and with the new growth and tender shoots, buds, fruit and small animals that must be sought in more southerly climes with the onset of fall.

For other forms of birdlife, the coming of autumn means a diet of nuts, seeds from trees, weeds and even scattered grain in the wake of harvesting in nearby fields.

Even in winter, our forests and woodlands provide a surprising abundance of conifer seeds, weed seeds and berries sticking up through the snow, as well as insects hibernating in the trunks of trees. It is then that we see birds like the white-breasted nuthatch in the woodlands, working their way, head-first, down the trunks of trees, pecking and poking the bark for sleeping insects. Nuthatches do not migrate and, when food is scarce, can sometimes be lured to feeding stations to feed on seed and suet along with their lookalikes, the chickadees.

Take a winter walk through any woodlot and you will almost certainly be rewarded with the sound of woodpeckers and perhaps sapsuckers tap-tap-tapping the trees in search of food. Each season brings its own delights.

Because of the availability of blossoms and flowers from ground level to treetop, and because of the many small insects there, even hummingbirds can generally be found near woodlands in many areas; because they prefer to nest in coniferous trees or in open woods close by farming country, so can certain species of dove. Our forests are also home to birds of prey such as owls, which are attracted there by the many small animals that make up a large part of their diet.

Throughout North America, our forests and woodlands, as well as being alive with the sounds of jays, ravens and numerous species of songbirds and perching birds, are home to game birds such as grouse, partridge and some species of quail. The forest provides protection as well as food; all of the forest birds, in addition to their protective coloring, exhibit considerable skill at disappearing into the spruce, cedar and forest undergrowth in quick, short bursts of flight.

In order to truly enjoy the birds and other creatures that dwell in the woods, one must stop and stand very still. Then, and only then, will the forest come alive with sound.

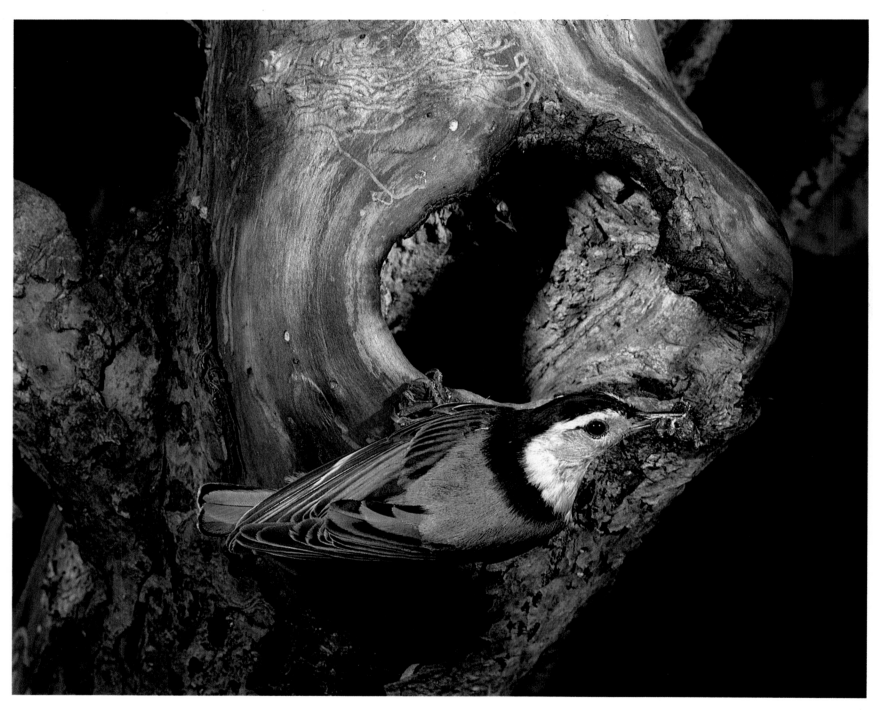

Page 76. The clearly enunciated "chick-a-dee-dee-dee," the black cap, black bib and white cheeks are the trademarks of the frisky black-capped chickadee.

Above. Similar in coloring to the chickadee, the white-breasted nuthatch can often be seen travelling headfirst down the trunks of trees in winter, searching the bark for hibernating insects and insect eggs.

Breeding in thickets and shrubbery,
the brown thrasher hides its nest deep
within hedges and close to the ground.
Like the robin, it can frequently be
seen feeding on lawns, where it digs
for insects with its long bill.

Above. As aggressive and bold as it is beautiful, the blue jay is also extremely inquisitive and noisy. Its diet includes insects, grain, fruit, acorns and sometimes the eggs and nestlings of other birds.

Right. Sometimes called the gray jay, the Canada jay is a curious and often bold visitor to campgrounds, picnic sites or wherever food scraps are likely to be found.

Left. The most common of all wood-peckers in the eastern U.S.A. and Canada, the small downy searches the bark of trees for wood-boring ants and caterpillars. It can also be lured to feeding stations with suet and seeds.

Above. A much darker bird than the blue jay, the Steller's jay will occasionally move out of its coniferous or mixed-wood forest habitat to live in orchards or gardens.

From Alaska to the central United
States, and from coast to coast, the
ruffed grouse is a hardy species, able
to survive even the worst of winters
because of its ability to find food above
snow level. Its spring mating routine,
the "drumming" pictured here, is
frequently heard but seldom seen.

Its tail and its small size distinguish the white-tailed ptarmigan. It also differs in its habitat, preferring alpine meadows and mountain slopes to the arctic tundra.

Well camouflaged in all seasons, the willow ptarmigan is all but invisible against the arctic snow. This arctic grouse is a tundra dweller, and both the male and female take on winter coloring.

Above. The beautiful iridescent coloring of the ruby-throated hummingbird is particularly noticeable when the bird hovers, its tiny insect-like wings beating between 3,500 and 4,500 times a minute.

Right. Despite its tiny size, approximately one-tenth of an ounce, the calliope hummingbird frequently dives on birds much larger than itself, and when protecting its young has been known to chase squirrels away from the nesting tree.

Upper left. A male Franklin's or spruce grouse displays its magnificent courting plumage. An inhabitant of coniferous forests and woodlots, this game bird is so tame that it can be studied at close range.

Lower left. The small, chicken-like California quail sports a forward-curved plume and exquisite facial markings. Unlike the grouse, it is not adapted to feeding above the snow cover, and frequently suffers during the winter for want of food.

Right. Strikingly handsome and noisy, the red-headed woodpecker feeds on flying insects, wild fruit and acorns as well as insects found in rotting trees; it will even sometimes take the eggs and young of other birds.

Previous pages. Similar to the crow in appearance except for its larger size and ruffled throat feathers, the common raven is the largest passerine, or perching, bird in the world. Here a pair practice the lazy, graceful aerial acrobatics for which they are well known.

Above. Distinguished by its bill color and by a bright red ring around its eye, the black-billed cuckoo feeds almost entirely on caterpillars. Here an adult tends a hungry youngster in the nest.

Right. The hairy woodpecker is common to woodland areas across Canada. Like other woodpeckers, its sturdy, vertical body and thick-boned skull are eminently suited to climbing the trunks and branches of trees to drill out the wood-boring insects that are its food.

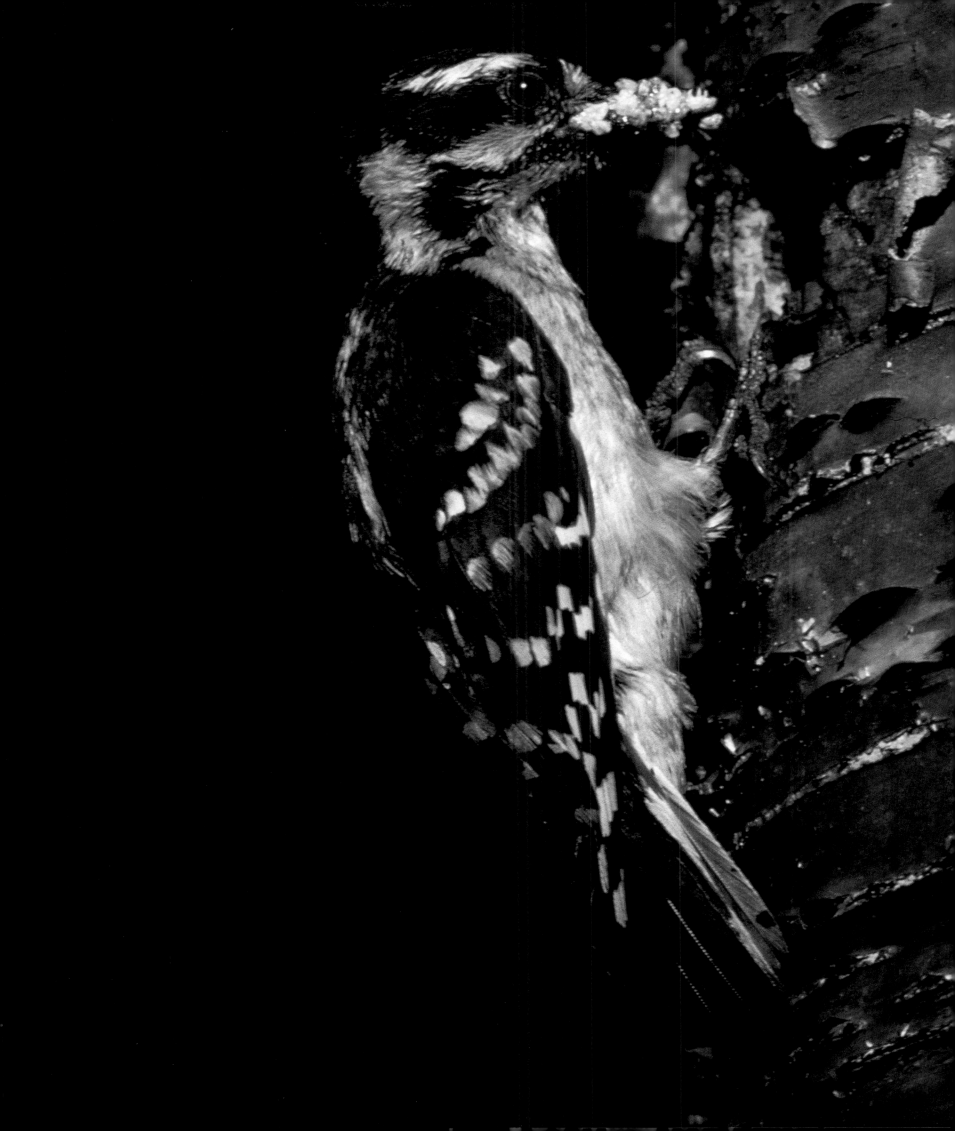

SHORE BIRDS

Surrounded by ocean on all sides, criss-crossed by streams and rivers and dotted with lakes of every size, the North American continent provides a wide range of habitat for the many species of shore, marsh and wading birds that live here. Our coastal waters teem with fish and other forms of marine life, while cliffs and rocky beaches along the ocean's edge provide nesting sites close by. Rivers, lakes and other inland waterways, as well as being rich with food, offer the added protection of camouflage in the vegetation growing on small islands or along their banks. Spring flooding in many areas creates great stretches of marshland, thereby giving birth to excellent nesting, breeding and feeding areas for the many species of bird-life that thrive on insects, amphibians, reptiles and small fish. Salt marshes as well, often formed at the mouths of large rivers where they flow into the sea, are home to a wide variety of wading birds.

From the smallest sandpiper, measuring just over four inches in length, to the great blue heron which stands four feet tall and has a wingspan of up to six feet, each of the birds within this fascinating group is specially adapted to its surroundings.

Many waders, like some members of the sandpiper family, are low-tide feeders that sleep when the tide is high, while others, like the sanderling, can often be seen running in small groups at the edge of the waves.

Turnstones, true to their name, search for their food along rocky beaches by turning over stones and pebbles with their bills to get at the small marine animals underneath.

The American avocet, on the other hand, slices its bill back and forth through soft mud in search of small worms, while the oystercatcher probes the sand for bivalves which it then cracks with its strong bill.

Larger waders, like the heron, have longer legs that enable them to stalk small fish, water snakes and frogs which they spear with their long, sharp beaks in the shallow waters of lakes, ponds or marshes.

The American bittern exhibits a remark-able camouflage, both with the vertical mark-ings of its plumage which match the marsh reeds and grasses where it nests and with its instinct to point its long bill straight up into the air when in danger, thereby blending more completely into its surroundings.

The wading birds are among nature's great-est travellers, some sandpipers, snipes and plovers being known to travel upwards of 16,000 kilometres (10,000 miles) on the annual flights between their northern breed-ing grounds and their winter homes on the other side of the globe.

Page 94. The enormous nest of the great blue heron, often up to three feet across, is repaired and added to year after year. Here, a pair of adult birds survey the world around them.

Above. With stealthy, deliberate steps, a green-backed heron stalks the water's edge for small fish or insects. About the size of a crow, this magnificently colored bird sports a crest that lifts when the heron is startled.

Right. The great blue heron can measure up to four feet in height, with a wingspan of six feet. An expert hunter, it can often be seen pursuing fish, frogs and water snakes, which it expertly stabs in shallow water with swift jabs of its pointed bill.

Previous pages. Looking bewildered by the world around them, two young green-backed herons stand in their nest as they await the return of their parents. It will be some weeks before they join the adult birds in the business of gathering food.

Above. Four young American bitterns appear to await the hatching of a fifth member of the family in their marshland habitat.

Right. An American bittern eyes the camera in its classic "freeze" position, its bill pointed skyward, its color and stripes blending into the marsh reeds, making it remarkably invisible.

Previous pages. Sanderlings appear to be practicing precision drill as they run along a sandy beach, following the waves up and down the shore in search of food.

Above. Sometimes measuring up to seven-and-a-half inches, the thin "sickle-bill" of the long-billed curlew is used to hunt for this wading bird's diet of insects, small fish and larvae.

More often heard than seen, the small
Virginia rail seldom flies, preferring
instead to run through rushes and
marshgrass where it feeds on insects
and small fish.

Above. Generally preferring rocky shores to sandy beaches, the purple sandpiper is one of about fifteen species of small and medium-sized sandpipers commonly seen in eastern North America.

Right. A large member of the sandpiper family, the marbled godwit spends its summers feeding and nesting along the marshy shores of either salt or fresh water and its winters in South America.

Left. The smallest of the sandpipers, the least sandpiper is also one of the tamest, and can be easily approached in its natural habitat. Here an adult tends its camouflaged eggs.

Above. A colonial nester, the black-crowned night heron roosts during the day, usually in trees near the marsh or swampland where it will arrive promptly at dusk to begin feeding on fish, frogs and mice.

Appropriately named for its colorful legs, the lesser yellowlegs often submerges its whole head when chasing after small fish and aquatic insects in shallow water.

The slender, up-turned bill, long legs
and striking colors are the unmistakable features of this American avocet
tending her nest. The nest, usually
built in a ground depression near
water, is lined with grass and weeds.

Left. The most numerous of our shore-birds, the semipalmated sandpiper derives its name from its partially-webbed toes, an unusual feature in this family. It feeds on low-tide beaches and rests when the tide is high.

Above. The double black band across its breast is the unmistakable marking of the killdeer. So, too, is the spirit this bird will put into her "broken-wing act" to lure predators away from her young.

113

Previous pages. Extremely social, even in breeding season, the American coot nests and feeds in small colonies. Its diet is largely insects and aquatic plants, though it may occasionally wander onto land for grass or sprouting grain.

Above. The American woodcock builds its nest on the ground, where it sleeps during the day; it feeds at night, mostly on earthworms. Here an adult settles onto four eggs.

Legendary for its migratory flights of some 9,000 miles, including approximately 2,400 miles over open ocean, the American golden plover here shows off its striking spring plumage.

A group of ruddy turnstones share a
rocky perch with two whimbrels. The
turnstone is named for its habit of
upturning stones and beach pebbles
in search of the invertebrates on which
it feeds.

Sometimes referred to as Wilson's snipe, the common snipe is an easy bird to confuse with the woodcock because of its size, coloring and long, straight bill.

WATER BIRDS

Water birds are a rather gregarious lot, often preferring the company of the flock to a solitary existence. There are more than 140 species of ducks, geese and swans in the world. They are readily recognizable, with their short legs, curious webbed feet and their comic waddling gait.

One of this country's best-loved birds is the Canada goose. Anyone fortunate enough to have heard its migratory honking and witnessed the great V-formations as the geese head south from their Arctic breeding grounds will not soon forget the sight. The ornamental plumage of the waterfowl— especially that of the harlequins, redheads and the spectacular hooded mergansers—is also admired for its beauty.

Like the ducks, geese and swans, many other birds are well-adapted to life on our oceans, great inland lakes and other waterways. Pelicans and cormorants live entirely on fish, each taking them in their own unique way.

As well as their spectacular dives for fish swimming near the surface of the ocean, large groups of pelicans are sometimes seen swimming and feeding in formation, beating their enormous wings on the water as they chase large schools of fish into the shallows. Cormorants, by contrast, also dive, but then pursue their prey by swimming after it under water, catching it from behind.

Loons, like cormorants, catch fish by swimming after them, but make their legendary dives from the surface of the water and not from the air. Loons supplement their diet with frogs, shellfish and vegetation.

Murres, which are the northern equivalent of the penguin, nest in large colonies on rocky cliffs in the northern reaches of both the Atlantic and Pacific oceans. Each pair produces a single egg. Two to three weeks after hatching, the young join their parents at sea where they winter and feed at the edge of the Continental Shelf.

Gannets too are colonial nesters, their springtime nesting antics and territorial quarrelling making them a favorite of many serious bird-watchers. Perhaps the most beautiful of all seabirds is the puffin, a most amazing and colorful sight in the lonely ocean.

Page 120. During migration, the plump, handsome snow goose stops to feed and rest at fresh or saltwater marshes, at lakes and often in grainfields.

Previous pages. The snow goose lays between three and five white to creamy eggs on the ground, and lines its nest of moss and weeds with its own down.

Above. The tiny American tree sparrow nests in the Arctic, heading south in the winter, when it can often be seen with other sparrows and juncos around feeding stations or feeding on seed pods of dried weeds.

A Canada goose turns its eggs. The nest, built in a hollow in the ground, is made from plants and is well lined with down.

Extremely social, American white pelicans feed, roost, fly and nest in flocks. Feeding in formation, they will swim side by side, beating their wings on the water to chase schools of fish into the shallows.

American white pelicans are a photographer's delight, especially when roosting.

One of these young American white pelicans is just beginning to get its white feathers; their rudimentary-looking nest is a depression in the earth with debris gathered at its rim.

Smaller than the arctic or common
loon, and with a distinct upward tilt
to its bill, the red-throated loon is the
only loon that can fly from land as well
as from water.

The common loon builds its nest in
reeds near the water, usually on small
islands, and not infrequently on top of
a muskrat house.

Above. Because of the remoteness of its summer nesting and feeding ground, few people get to see the magnificent arctic loon in its natural habitat.

Right. Seldom seen inland, the black-legged kittiwake nests in colonies along the rocky North Atlantic coast and spends most of its time at sea, where it feeds on fish and other marine life.

The redhead frequents shallow, fresh water at the edges of lakes, even along the seacoast. This duck takes its name from the male's winter and breeding plumage.

After wintering in the southern United States and South America, the small blue-winged teal is one of the last pond ducks to arrive back in the northern breeding grounds.

Taking its name from the two elongated tail-feathers which extend upward from its rump, the pintail is one of our most elegant and graceful ducks, both on the water and in flight.

Commonly referred to as the baldpate, the American widgeon seems to prefer feeding at night, spending the daylight hours bobbing about on open water or in reeds.

Previous pages. A popular summer visitor to freshwater lakes throughout the northern United States and Canada, the common merganser is a fish-eating, diving duck. Like all mergansers, when in flight, the head, neck and body form a straight line.

Above. This young mallard duck, being looked after by its mother until it learns to fly, will also learn to forage in shallow water, not by diving but by dipping from the surface with its tail pointing straight up to the sky.

Above. Northern gannets lay a single egg, rarely two, in a nest of seaweed on a level surface at the edge of a cliff. After hatching, the young learn to fly from the cliff face at about 12 weeks.

Following pages. Nesting in colonies along the rocky coast, the northern gannet is a close relative of the pelican, although it does not have the pelican's larger bill.

Left. Somewhat larger than the double-crested cormorant, the great cormorant can often be seen standing on a rock or piling with its wings half opened, drying its plumage in the sun.

Above. A familiar sight along the Atlantic coast, where it sits on the pilings of wharves, on breakwaters and often on marker buoys, the double-crested cormorant lives entirely on fish.

The oldsquaw is a seaduck found
along both coasts of North America
and on the Great Lakes. A magnificent
diver, it feeds on fish, crustaceans and
mollusks at depths of up to 200 feet.

Dives of up to 30 feet, for the succulent roots of underwater plants, are not uncommon for the canvasback, largest of the game ducks.

The hand-painted look of the male harlequin duck's black, blue, chestnut and white plumage makes it a photographer's delight.

Left. Rarely sighted in the wild, the gadwall nonetheless is the most widely distributed of all ducks, breeding in North America, Europe, Asia and even parts of Africa.

Above. The smallest of the diving ducks, the chubby bufflehead, sometimes called the butterball, is recognizable by the iridescence of the purple and green tints, especially on the head of the male.

Above. The only pond duck to nest off the ground, the crested wood duck makes its nest in a natural cavity high up in the trunk or in a rotting limb of a tree near water.

Right. Nesting in the arctic and moving south in winter, the parasitic jaeger feeds on small mammals, smaller birds and their eggs, fish and carrion.

The glaucous gull is a large and busy predator, robbing ducks and other gulls of their catch and frequently feeding on the young of many nesting birds.

Named for the black ring near the tip of its beak, the ring-billed gull can frequently be spotted on golf courses or following a farmer's tractor for insects turned up by the plow.

A young ring-billed gull emerges from an egg in its nest. The nest, built on the ground, is made of grass and weeds and, frequently, rubbish.

This mew gull's graceful, soaring flight is a wonder to behold. One of the smaller gulls, the mew can often be seen feeding with larger gulls along the coast.

Left. The beautiful Atlantic puffin, nick-named the "sea parrot," breeds on remote coastal islands from Newfoundland to Maine.

Upper right. The small black tern, a graceful inhabitant of inland lakes and marshes, feeds mainly on aquatic insects which it catches while flying.

Lower right. Like all phalaropes, the Wilson's phalarope is sometimes called the swimming sandpiper and it frequently feeds while swimming in small circles. As with the red-necked, the female is more brightly colored than the male.

Following pages. The common murre lays one egg on the bare rock of an oceanside cliff or rocky island. In winter, it is strictly a marine species, feeding in the coastal waters to the edge of the continental shelf.

Above. The long-distance travels of the arctic tern, twice-yearly flights between arctic and antarctic waters, make it a legend in the world of birds.

Right. A diving duck found largely in western North America, the puffy-headed Barrow's goldeneye lays as many as a dozen eggs, usually in tree hollows or cavities in rocks.

Following page. Among the few birds that reverse the sex roles, it is the female red-necked phalarope who has the brightest plumage, who initiates courtship and who, after laying the eggs, leaves the male to raise the young.

PHOTO CREDITS

INDEX